DIRTY SNOW

DIRTY SNOW

POEMS BY
Tom Wayman

HARBOUR PUBLISHING

Harbour Publishing Co. Ltd.
P.O. Box 219, Madeira Park, BC, V0N 2H0
www.harbourpublishing.com

Cover photograph by Frank Leung/iStockphoto
Title page photo by Mary Bailey
Cover design by Anna Comfort O'Keeffe
Text design by Mary White
Printed and bound in Canada

Harbour Publishing acknowledges financial support from the Government of Canada through the Canada Book Fund and the Canada Council for the Arts, and from the Province of British Columbia through the BC Arts Council and the Book Publishing Tax Credit.

Library and Archives Canada Cataloguing in Publication

Wayman, Tom, 1945–
    Dirty snow / Tom Wayman.

Poems.
ISBN 978-1-55017-586-8

    1. Afghan War, 2001- --Poetry. I. Title.

PS8595.A9D57 2012   C811'.54   C2012-900329-8

"The war had dirtied the snow."

—Roch Carrier, *La Guerre, Yes Sir!*
(trans. Sheila Fischman)

CONTENTS

THE EFFECT OF THE AFGHAN WAR ON THE LANDSCAPES AND PEOPLE OF SOUTHEASTERN BRITISH COLUMBIA

MY WOUNDS

CALLING THE SEASON HOME

THE EFFECT OF THE AFGHAN WAR ON THE LANDSCAPES AND PEOPLE OF SOUTHEASTERN BRITISH COLUMBIA

"It's hard to be a poet in wartime. We're used now to the corruption of language by the corporations and government: every price or fare increase is an 'adjustment,' and, in my area of BC, logging roads have become 'fibre extraction routes.' So the debasement of language in war is no longer a surprise.

"But during Canada's intervention in the Afghan civil war, one could go days without hearing any reference to our involvement. Not a word from politicians or the media, unless a Canadian happened to be killed. Often that event was only given a tiny mention on the news, quickly replaced by the far-more-important latest antics of some vacuous entertainment celebrity. The silence, at least for people like poets used to language describing the world, was deafening . . ."

INTEREST

"You may not be interested in war,
but war is interested in you."
—Alan Furst, misattributed to Leon
Trotsky

You're not interested in considering
        the war—*The government knows best,*
        or *What can you expect from those clowns*—
        but the war has seized
        your interest, and some of the capital, too,
        from your taxes not spent
        on medical equipment, road repaving,
        housing for the poor, libraries. These rows and rows of dollars
        have been conscripted
        —heroes all, once in uniform
        and sent away to kill
        and die. Nobody ever asks
the enemy to pay for
the bullets, shells, bombs and missiles
you generously donate toward them.

You're not interested in
        mentioning the war, yet to relatives and friends

of ones killed by fire from a tank
operated by soldiers with the name of your nation
on their sleeves, you killed them. You drove others
out of their homes, or levelled their houses
while they were absent. The survivors are interested
in why you want them dead. You object:
What people on Earth
have control over what their government does
but the high-tech boots of troops
patrolling through a village of mud and straw
make the sound of your name as they pass.

You're not interested
but the young men and women from your town
blown up by improvised mines
or incoming rocket-propelled grenades
or destroyed by friendly fire
are saviours, your government says:
they tried to keep you safe,
convinced you were feeling imperilled, or they defended
a list of intangibles wrapped carefully in your flag,
or they risked their lives to protect
the good inhabitants of whatever country or
tribal region they were occupying
while they were alive. These dead
were interested enough in the war
once they arrived at it
to die there, and the government says
they bravely perished, even the suicides,
the drunks, the newbies, and
those issued faulty equipment. The men and women
and children they killed before they died
also died for you
though these were not courageous and noble
but bad people, or misguided,
or just unfortunate, and though you were not
interested.

"Acknowledged or not, the Afghan conflict became part of the background to daily life. Although mostly unspoken, this omnipresence of war mirrors how in the Selkirk Mountains of southeastern BC where I live, the turn of the seasons and the work that changes with the seasons is all-pervasive . . ."

ROSES AT THE GRAVE OF SUMMER

The mountain stream, year after year,
    washes soil downslope to the valley floor
    leaving behind a creek bed of
    stones.

    At Lebahdo Flats
cows graze in the morning fog
as the school bus passes.

        By dusk, the air
is heavy with the coming winter.
Damp earth clings to the shovel blade
and pitchfork. The tools
clang together before being placed
to lean again against the inside of the shed.

Where the house wall
faces east across the valley
    Joseph's Coat roses—barren since August—
blossom a last time.

"As the war dragged on year after year, even the magnificence of our mountain home did not escape, at least for me, being saturated with that unseen presence . . ."

MT. GIMLI PASHTUN

I

At the start, the trail pushes through alder thickets
    along a creek, then crosses the stream bed
    on two logs with metal mesh affixed for grip. After that
    the path is relentless in its climb: switchback
    after switch-
    back up the wooded ridge,
                    boot by boot
    also scrambling under a fallen trunk
    or over as huckleberries
    swell along the steep route, the forest's species
    changing. The trail eventually lifts amid
    rock ledges, cone-shaped alpine fir
    and stunted brush

                    while the immense black mound
    of Gimli's summit
    is visible between the trees—krummholz branches
    shrivelled by the snows, Engelmann spruce boughs
    seared and malformed by frost—

until the woods are gone: the path traverses
an open country
of tilted inclines of dusty earth
and stones, sparse grass tufts. The route
ambles around and atop boulders
of a scree slope, the trail marked by
low stacks of rocks.

Beside the path,
the mountainside falls away
into a drainage below: a slanted field of tundra,
a few clusters of evergreens,
two ponds. Pika watch, squeak and
dart. Gimli's granite ridge
fills the horizon to the north, three hundred metres aloft.
At the eastern end of the cornice, the summit mass
rears a further thousand metres.

II

A loss thrums in the soil here,
vibrates in the cold alpine wind.

Here the Pashtuns blown apart, or maimed
by bullets released in the name of this country

now dwell,
together with the uniformed young men

shuffled into earth in a box
borne by eight of their own, or returned to us

alive but changed.
All that grows
in this harsh silence of stones

grows in the scant weeks clear of snow:
roots reach to grasp a mountain

of black dust. To the east, south, west,
serried bells of blued peaks

—chop of shore-broken waves—
toll through the emptiness.

Those who rule us have sent
men and women with our money

and in our name
to kill to protect a corruption

struggling against another corruption. Our lawmakers
have proclaimed as enemy

a force our side once armed to destroy
a third corruption, whose politicians promised,

as do those who now hold the capital,
to pave roads, build schools for women,

curtail opium shipments.
                              When a bear

        stands on the trail to block the way,
        her head lifted, tilting side to side

        to scent us, or black fur is abruptly evident
        descending the slope

        toward us, the future
we are given

cannot be predicted or justified.
Achievements, skills, insights

mean nothing to the unreasonable menace
advancing in the icy air:

our government's insistence that they
—that we—have always represented virtue,

that our peaceful heritage
affords our troops the right

to establish fields of fire,
that torture, the stoning of apostates

and adulteresses are our ally's culture,
meriting respect, while our soldiers, each equipped

with expensive armour, communication
devices, night vision goggles, cunningly designed

weaponry, combat clothing and boots
are welcomed

by men and women whose bodies
are wrapped in ragged cloth, who lack shoes.

> The unfairness of the bear's power.
> No protest short of retreat
> or violence suffices
> to counter its presence in our lives.

III

An alien death has been brought
to these mountains. Foot patrols, tank squadrons,
radio calls for other men to kill from the air
—all bedecked with the symbols
of this country—echo among the peaks' vistas of
innumerable summits, roadless forest.

>   In the serenity
> above treeline
> a spreading stain bleaches half the sky.
> To the south, amid dim cloud-mounds,

are flashes of light: detonations
of an improvised
innocence.

—near Slocan, BC

"It seems to me we were rushed into this conflict. Our masters were eager to line up with US president George W. Bush's attempt to turn a crime—airline hijackings resulting in mass murder—into a war—the officially sanctioned form of mass murder. With scarcely a murmur of protest from the opposition benches in Parliament, we were hustled toward an invasion of Afghanistan . . ."

TRANSPORTS

Heavy rigs painted desert camo
careen along the two-lane,
convoys of three or four of the tractor-trailers

forming and dissipating
as they push forward through the line of traffic.
Most tractors tow a semi- plus pup-trailer

although several haul low-beds
onto which a Leopard tank is chained,
a canvas sleeve over the muzzle,

or flat-decks bearing a tarpaulined shipment.
Each cab features a deep-drop external visor
that shadows the driver from sight,

an after-market array of running lamps,
and a small flag painted just above the grille
—tiny stain of red and white

preceding the blur of brown.
Licence plates either are missing
or display a series of numbers

below the name of this country.
One flat black bumper
swells to fill the rear-view

of a civilian sedan.
The rig that crowds it, approaching a curve,
sways out to cross a double yellow line

and accelerates, rocking the vehicle being passed
as trailers weave erratically
before the tractor bulls back into the other lane,

the overtaken car braking hard
to prevent being side-swiped
while an oncoming Reimer B-train blasts its horn

as it evades a collision
only by steering onto the shoulder,
dust plume rising from gravel

until tires shudder back onto asphalt
and the B-train vanishes behind. Already
the grille of another military tractor

occupies the rear window of the car
while the rig in the lead
speeds down a clear stretch of highway,

confident no risk is unworthy
of its mission: to race to a terminal,
fastened to the load of death it carries now

through an indifferent wood.

"Ordinary life has enough sorrows and regrets, I believe, without a community or nation needing to seek out armed combat . . ."

THE SUMMER HAS FLARED

and dimmed: bracken now yellow
and brown, hazel leaves
mainly dusty gold, speckles of that colour
also visible in the green plumes of birch,
poplar, cottonwood. A late September silence
has permeated the valley
this afternoon. Down the lane that skirts the base of the ridge

two *For Sale* signs linger from May: one home on its acreage
curtainless, with no vehicles, stack of firewood
or trailered boat in its yard.
The other place still evidently lived in. Over two decades
I have watched these signs appear and evaporate
like snow. Already today our fields, gardens, forests
have travelled through showers, broken clear into

sunlight, and now pass beneath
overlays of whitish-grey clouds. I hope I never know
my house sold and empty, never have to drive or be driven a last time
along the river remembering the August night I first arrived here
at the wheel of a rented cube van. I don't want ever to follow a truck
that hauls my belongings
out between these valley walls.

*"Poll after poll showed a majority of Canadians opposed to our
military engagement in Afghanistan. And no wonder. The government
poured millions upon millions of dollars, and squandered the lives and
bodies and minds of hundreds of Canadians and thousands of Afghans,
in propping up a corrupt narco-administration in Kabul that could
not survive without the presence of a continually increasing number
of foreign troops. This consortium of warlords and druglords was
opposed by a Pashtun tribal movement of religious fundamentalists,
women-hating and women-fearing, whom our side not so long before
had armed and trained to overthrow a different narco-administration
that, in fact, didn't endure without the presence of large numbers of
foreign troops. Both sides in the most recent civil war have been heavily
involved in the heroin trade that wreaks such havoc in Canada's inner
cities. The money spent in Canada's blundering efforts to intervene on
the side of one of two equally odious combatants is money that was
not available for Canadian health care, for Canadian post-secondary
education, for Canadian social welfare of every kind.*

*"The stupidity, shame and waste resulting from military
participation in this civil war has dozens of parallels with the US
intervention in another civil war in Asia decades ago, the Vietnam
War . . ."*

THE GHOST OF LYNDON BAINES JOHNSON APPEARS AS GUEST OF HONOUR AT A RAMP CEREMONY FOR THREE MORE SLAIN CANADIAN SOLDIERS

1.

Drone of two bagpipes
from the blackness. Then the first mingled tones
send "The Green Hills of Tyrol," also titled
"A Scottish Soldier," across a floodlit area of
Kandahar Airfield
where six hundred men and women in desert camo
are drawn up in lines on asphalt. Beyond the formation
a CC-130 Hercules is parked

22

with rear ramp down, the vast hold of the aircraft
open for cargo.

Facing the ranks,
on a reviewing stand both suits and uniforms
sit in the cooling night.

Now the bagpipes wheeze to silence. Muffled shouts
from the direction the music originated,
and the pipes hum again and squeal into "Amazing Grace." The
    musicians
step slowly from behind a building
toward the space between the dignitaries and assembled troops.
Trailing the pipes, three sets of uniformed pallbearers
pace in succession, carrying the long boxes
atop each of which is secured
a red and white flag.

The procession
halts before the stand, and the coffins
are lowered to the tarmac
side by side, one end pointing toward the airplane.
Another cry of command, and each burial party is brought to rigid
    attention,
the pallbearers facing each other across the containers.
The crowd of soldiers likewise jerks to a taut stance.

2.

On the stand, a bemedalled uniform approaches
the microphone. The device
is balky, its words fading and swelling, as the syllables
reverberate from the field's repair hangars,
terminal structure, clusters of tents:
a vibrating echo ricochets, something about
democracy . . . dying for freedom . . . their country. Then

after what might have been sentences of introduction,
the podium is yielded to a suited man with thinning grey hair
who towers over the mic, pausing before he speaks
to survey the scene before him.

The new voice
has a nasal quality, audible even through the metallic rasp
and resonation of the PA. The figure
appears to be relating how he *said on September 25, 1965,*
we don't want American boys to do the fighting
that Asian boys should do. We don't want to get tied down
in a land war in Asia. This is meant as prologue:
the tall grey-haired man continues to slowly explain himself
but the mic has picked up
a different transmission *um negative on that, Baker Seven. That's sector*
four niner foxtrot. Repeat: four niner foxtrot

This interruption is overlaid by a voice
talking for a full minute in what seems to be
Russian. After which, several phrases too faint to be heard
are followed by a heavily accented report *he tells to you*
that if you stop when Afghan police order stop,
they rob you. If you don't halt,
they kill you. At the podium
the tall man continues with his address,
yet another voice in Pashto
is heard, and also a different interpreter
the Messenger, may He be honoured forever,
instructs us uh girls are not to be educated, uh that such an act
is contrary to the holy word, thus uh is blasphemy,
and whoever blasphemes must die so the faithful
A burst of static, but on the reviewing stand
the mic has been claimed by
another individual in camo, with a white scarf
over his shoulders that extends
down the front of his battledress. The sound system
intones *His holy name*

The clergyman returns to his chair
as the bemedalled man resumes the mic.

3.

On the field, a shouted order. The burial units
stir, the boxes are gripped
and unevenly hoisted aloft to their proper altitude.
The clump of individuals on the reviewing stand
rises with the caskets. All salute,
along with the rows of soldiers,
as the bagpipes shriek back to life:
this time, "O Canada." Several bars into the anthem,
at another yell, the boxes lurch into motion
behind the pipers, who step solemnly
across the distance to the ramp
and up it, as after them the assigned detachments
bear the dead, the flag
of their country, the country itself
into the yawning dark.

"Dreams, some say, are where what we suppress in our waking existence finds expression. How has the everyday silence wrapped around the Afghan War affected Canada's *dreams?*

"Even in the profound peace of night at my country home, dreams arise that try to speak to me, but in a language I do not always comprehend . . ."

PROCESSION

The valley is a dark river.
An occasional pock of light
flecks the blackness that purls against the
base of these ranges:
a solitary porch lamp
or yard light
surrounded by black fields,
stands of forest. Or a thin beam weaves
along a dark trace of
highway: a late-running tractor-trailer,
or pickup.
The shape of a house looms
in an eddy of the valley night
and within that dwelling
I lie on a black bed
breathing out the night's stillness,
breathing in darkness
that lowers me
onto a sandy road between meadows
—a route I walk
accompanied by four figures
holding a *chuppah* above me,
the canopy worn through in spots,
its fringe tattered. Two of the pole-bearers
I dimly recognize—somebody from my past
I cannot name, if I ever knew
who he was, and a similar

half-familiar face
from my present. The others
are unknown: one clearly glimpsed,
but, like his companions,
gazing with an intent expression at the crest
the road slopes toward, eyes uninterested in
me. The fourth's face is blurred
as we advance, feet lifting
a low mist of dust.

"Despite the bizarre situation of living in a nation at war that most of the time tried to pretend no such conflict was happening, people became accustomed to this kind of existence. One of humanity's strengths is the ability to adapt to almost anything . . ."

ADJUSTMENT

Perhaps the moon wearied of
metal objects that landed on it
with charring flames

or, more likely, the satellite grew tired of being endlessly jostled
by the opposing pulls of gravity and centrifugal force

but one night an astronomer observed
aberrations in its orbit
Over six months, the evidence became conclusive
—the immense rocky sphere
was slowly descending toward Earth
like an enormous airship settling lower
like the deliberate closing of
the lid of a box

Once the moon began to loom larger by the week
panic flared among inhabitants of the globe
desperate to know where the errant sphere would hit
Calculations eventually yielded the point of impact
as the middle of the Gulf of Georgia
between southern Vancouver Island and the mainland

With the moon filling half the sky
the Gulf and San Juan Islands were evacuated
before the gigantic mass
could crush forests, mountains, villages
Entire coastal cities—Seattle, Tacoma, Vancouver, Victoria
—in addition to smaller settlements along

Puget Sound, the Olympic Peninsula
and Georgia Strait were also emptied
as a precaution against flooding
The sphere pushing into the lower atmosphere
began to glow red from air resistance
Dire predictions that ranged from deadly clouds of scalding steam
to the Earth breaking apart as a consequence of the impending collision
preoccupied the news media
while the highest tides ever recorded
poured over breakwaters and seawalls
to strand vessels high up on beaches
even on the far side of the Pacific

Yet the moon touched down so gently
its displacement of millions of tonnes of sea water
that surged west down the Strait of Juan de Fuca
and east toward the Fraser River delta
resulted in much-reduced loss of life
and did remarkably little damage
compared to the authorities' forecasts

The moon's bulk, however
completely blocked the former shipping channels
serving Puget Sound and the BC mainland
Views westerly from these shores
that had offered pleasing vistas
of ocean, clouds, distant snow-tipped mountains
now were obscured by a stupendous cratered dome
of greyish-white rock

The economic consequences
of the moon's descent
were daunting: besides the cleanup on land
the stream of container vessels to and from the Orient
had to be rerouted around Vancouver Island's stormy north cape
to a new port constructed on a fjord
hundreds of kilometres northwest of Vancouver

to which expensive rail and highway links
had to be built

           Some of these costs
were offset by an expansion in
tourism: everyone on the planet with the financial resources
wanted to visit the moon
Until the extraterrestrial arrival was declared
a World Heritage Site, entrepreneurs secured leases from
various federal, regional or local governments claiming jurisdiction
and dozens of waterfront holiday resorts were carved
out of the newcomer's dusty slopes
Meanwhile, the removal of the moon from orbit
resulted in the end of tidal ebb and flow
with disastrous consequences globally for
thousands of shellfish, crustacean and food fish
enterprises and their dependent communities
Scientists speculated whether the huge mass
now adhering to the Earth
would affect planetary spin and orbital progression
in unknown ways harmful to human life
or to the rest of the biosphere

           Yet the world
despite its bulging appendage
continued to steadily rotate on its axis
—although, according to experts
one-twenty-fifth of a minute slower than previously
Many people found the night sky
more beautiful in the absence of the moon
since each day of the month all the seasonal constellations were visible
shining among the other stars
between which the freshly burdened Earth
continued to journey
as it did around its indifferent and self-consuming sun

"One of the goofier aspects of the Afghan (and Iraqi) invasions is how US and Canadian financial experts who pronounce endlessly on the state of the North American economy and the factors that have affected it never mention the billions of dollars the Asian wars have cost. But the ridiculousness doesn't end there . . ."

THERE IS NO WAR, AND YOU WOULD NOT HAVE TO CONSIDER IT IF THERE WAS

You see, dollars spent on
whatever our armed forces have undertaken in Afghanistan
or anyplace else are not ordinary dollars.
Because this money is allotted for completely different purposes
than the usual government spending on
agricultural development, commuter trains, or
consumer protection agencies, this cash flow
does not arise from taxation, nor does it involve
fiscal activity in the standard sense
used to calculate, for example, GNP. Such peace or
security funds, including everything from weapons procurement
to repatriation of remains
and future veterans' care facilities, in fact evaporate retroactively
the moment these dollars are spent
and therefore generate zero impact on the economy,
let alone budgetary surpluses or deficits.

You see, too, Afghans have a proud warrior culture.
You'll recall this fact from the news stories when our allies were arming,
training and supplying the tribal groups
that now, sadly, have become the enemy
or at best are indifferent to the fate of the present tribal inhabitants of
the National Palace, who require an ever-increasing number
of our troops, and those of our coalition partners,
to protect Kabul from other tribal alignments among
the resolute fighters who comprise—leaving aside women and children—
that portion of the population not unfortunately freezing or starving to death

as they watch the convoys of ammunition
pass through their villages or along the roads,
or not busy raising the one stable cash crop
all sides encourage and purchase: the poppies
whose residue eventually is detected
in the veins of deceased inhabitants of certain urban districts
in our own country
—thus demonstrating that while the balance of casualties
inflicted by our soldiers or theirs currently may be tilted in our favour,
the comparative statistics are not yet complete
regarding collateral non-combatant deaths.

And speaking of fatalities, remember that the tragedy of
Canadians killed by firefights or improvised land mines
only occurs because the insurgents
are doing their job. Wait, that's wrong:
our soldiers are the ones
who, as they stress in media interviews,
have a job to do. Armed individuals on the opposing side, you see,
by contrast are devious and malicious,
display no regard for human life
and, despite lacking any airborne logistical or tactical capabilities
and bolstered by foreign personnel
who have no right to intervene in
Afghanistan's domestic affairs,
are determined to impose by force
a set of alien values
on an abject and defenceless people.

"The goal of every war is to terrify an enemy into submission—into agreeing to demands that they alter their behaviour in some way. So launching a 'War on Terror' is completely nonsensical, like advocating hatred toward hate . . ."

THE TERROR

after Denise Levertov

If this is wartime,
and that president "a wartime president," against what
is his power arrayed, are his prayers
composed?

       Crime, mass murder
pleads for the guilty's apprehension. But terror
is not vanquished by a shoulder-launched RPG
or an assault rifle. Neither will the armoured
Humvee, or the Bradley M2/M3 Fighting
Vehicle, carry us all to safety.

Surely applause for that president's war
arises from the old dread of Asia
where the jobs now devolve to
                         or could, whose strange citizens
are permitted to clamber into town, transform
the blocks we live in
             while among us, men and women
reap profit from these shifts, are not afraid,
                     even praise
the war, its opportunities.

          To assuage fear
is not the aim of retribution, but a goal of
justice. Preventative shunning, devices
that pierce darkness to "facilitate
interdiction of targets," that convert lentil fields to

no-go zones, do not defeat
terror, which can only be conquered
                                        by peace. *This war will* bring *peace,*
certain people always insist,
                            arming the poor,
the jobless. And the gods
—who each countenance among their minions
the invocation of terror
and hatred
                to intimidate, coerce, recruit—
laugh.

"An overseas military escapade is always a distraction from domestic problems. Part of the tragedy of a reckless or ill-considered war is that it exacerbates difficulties at home by consuming a nation's resources—material, financial, intellectual, psychological and more. Nor do the problems disappear, whether such a war is won or lost . . ."

HIGHWAY 6, EAST OF SLOCAN LAKE, DURING THE AFGHAN CAMPAIGN

Asphalt winds between the autumn's rust-coloured flagging
of the cedar limbs, the vivid gold and orange
of alder, cottonwood, birch
that blend with the greens of
balsam and spruce.

             The valley's forested walls
are speckled by feathery yellow larch
to the summits. Beauty
is the season's name, though highway maintenance
and snow-clearing
is now privatized: the profits of a few
seized from a need of all.
No one will reveal the numbers to demonstrate
how the current arrangement saves tax money
though this was the announced justification
for the change. Mist has lifted from the river
to float as streamers halfway up a slope
blotched by clear-cuts
among which thread sparse patches
of timber. The lakeside hospital
has been downgraded, most medical services
relocated two hours distant by ambulance. An AA club
every twenty klicks through this valley.
The dry land sort on the shore at Rosebery
abruptly closed, machine operators, tugboat crews
laid off. The railroad tracks torn up

a decade ago, so additional log haulers
crowd onto the route, bunch up behind
the house-sized chip trailers. The incessant passage of
the rigs' weighted wheels
press endless ruts into the pavement

where windrows of birch and poplar leaves
alongside exhale a sweet dusty fragrance
as the highway slows to navigate a corner
past a cutbank with miniature pines
rising from its sand. Ahead, the vista of gold and green
extends to a blue peak, to
Afghanistan.

"No sooner was the defeat of the Canadian armed forces in Afghanistan acknowledged, and the Canadian military occupation of that country scaled back, than the Canadian air force began bombing in Libya. The excuse given was that our government wanted to protect unarmed civilian protestors from attacks by Libyan authorities, even though Canada did not intervene when our ally, Saudi Arabia, similarly attacked unarmed protesters in Bahrain.

"In any case, the killing of Libyans—both those designated as bad people by our government, and those inadvertently blown up by Canadian pilots—resulted in, as did the Afghan War, a serious degradation of the quality of life of our communities."

AIR SUPPORT

A dropped school falls through air,
turning slowly as debris
pours from windows: a contrail of papers and books
streams upward thousands of metres
alongside computers, chairs, desks that tumble amid
woodworking equipment, lockers, maps,
basketballs, stage curtains

            all aimed
toward tiny huts far below—a brushy hillside's
cluster of subsistence farms
reportedly harbouring armed men: fenced yards
with a few chickens, one cow, an ancient horse eyeing
six rows of parched vegetables.

            Above the school
while it descends,
another follows, and beyond that, nearly invisible,
a third floats as the fighter-bomber arcs
away, and a second jet drones into position.
The pilot of the first, now on the mission's homeward leg,

reaches down in his cockpit
toward a thermos of hot coffee.

On the ground, hospitals released
in the initial attack wave
erupt sequentially into plumes of fire and dust
as the buildings land: operating tables,
obstetric wards, wheelchairs shatter into shrapnel,
the jagged particles racing outward amid the roiling smoke
to slice through mud walls, animal flesh, stone fences,
human lives that cling to the shaking
shuddering earth
while they clutch forty-year-old rifles
or axes, or the hand of a two-year-old
below the flash of wing
very distant
in the blue-and-white sky.

"The consequences of war do not end when the fighting stops, or, in the most recent case, when the last Canadian soldier leaves foreign soil . . ."

DIRTY SNOW

A spray of reddish dust: desiccated earth,
Shreds of maple, hardened blood.

Black particulate: charcoal,
Ash sifted across meadow, stream bank, road.

Tiny paper flakes: cream, blue, green—
Stems and serifs of numbers perceptible on the largest shards.

Mounds of detritus will linger if this snow melts.
What rain? What wind?

To what sea will the April runnels
Bear this pain?

MY WOUNDS

"The personalities of so many of us are at war within, as a consequence of trying to make sense of childhood, adolescence, adulthood even while we're in the midst of these experiences. You'd think that such endless internal *combat would satisfy whatever primal urges we retain to do battle externally with people around us . . ."*

MY WOUNDS

after Miguel Hernández

For the sin of fear
    the wound of loneliness

I loved the highway too much
    I made neither asphalt, bridges, nor the truck I drove
    But the night road said: *though you lose the fields*
    and the light
    I will carry you

For the sin of my fear
loneliness

I loved the fuzzed gold of October larch
    on the mountain
    the first glaze of green
    on birch sticks in April
    Mostly, I loved the wind
    in the empty air
    —a susurration chorusing
    from the guitars of the leaves
    from the throats of the river, the lodgepole pines

For my sin
my wound of love

I was continually afraid
    Behind the beach in the dense cedars

43

fresh mounds of graves
Her voice in the kitchen cutting herself from me
My voice choking into silence
whole lives for myself
for others

In a valley I loved and feared
I knelt in earth to place a row of radish seed
tomato seedlings
I pulled irrigation hoses across pastures
to release for hours
the water of loneliness

Who walked with me? Fear
Who sang to me? Wind
Who ran with me? Road

There was no wound like my wounds
        And they shone

"Even in peacetime, death shadows our lives. One of the devastating events that happens to us all in the normal course of life is the loss of a parent, then the other. I remember reading the see-sawing statistics from Afghanistan on which side killed the most civilians in a given month: the enemy, or ourselves. I doubt it was a comfort to any individual to think that at least their mother or father was shot or blown up by the forces of truth, justice and light . . ."

SNOW RIGHT TO THE WATER

I

Under white humps
where the forest
spills down low banks
to the corner of the lawn,
my exhausted parents sleep.
Nothing moves
in the late December day.
The austere cold
means the limbs of the evergreens
surrounding the house
are frosted, while on the ridge
and across fields
alder, birch, aspen bear
atop each branch and twig
thick blossoms of white.

           The only sound
is a distant snowplow grating south along the highway
on the valley's farther side.

           To be dead
is more tiring than the living imagine.
To assert yourself, remain a presence,
haunt through the yellowing spring,

hot winds of summer
requires energy the dead
barely possess—even if,
released from hibernation in March,
they are supposed to be rested.
By autumn, the strain
is evident: memory now
is reflexive, the dead merely
coast amid the weakened sun,
steadily descending leaves.

                    In winter
the dead are most dead
—this season of binaries
a manifestation closest to their own
state: white/black, chill/heated.
Even breath, even the passage of
we living across the Earth
is rendered visible. The dead, though,
my parents,
lie very still, at one
with the brittle world. Not breathing.
Insensate. Passive
despite blizzard, early dark,
frozen boughs snapped off.

II

On wires overlooking the marsh
near the bridge to the back road
an owl perches in the waning afternoon
to stare across the river

                    that rarely freezes,
that transports its icy fluid
toward an ocean whose shore is covered with snow
to the utmost edge of the tide.

"My mother died in 1995 and my father in 1999. I cannot shake the sense of loss . . ."

THE GROUSE THAT FLEW UNDERGROUND

My shovel cuts into brown soil:
    each slam of the blade under my boot
        chops roots, deflects off stones,

pries up gravelly earth
    to be carried to the surface and piled beside
        the ruffed grouse—eyelids closed

against the enormity
    of the day's changes: the bird strutting the lawn
        neck fanned outward, until it leaped aloft

to stutter through air to roost
    in the leafless birch. Then heaving itself
        into air once more toward a gap

in the wall of the house
    which reached out and struck it
        down amid the newly rising

iris shoots, tulip leaves already clipped short
    by the deer. Just within the forest gate
        I clear a path for the grouse:

an entrance my shovel hoists it into,
    feathered wings perfectly intact
        and ready to propel it

through the ground, to alight on buried roots
    and perch, to descend to pace atop bedrock,
        drumming to attract a mate,

then lift to flap ungainly across soil: a bird for my parents
　　to point out to each other
　　　　in their brown sky.

"I grew up connected to two families besides my own; their fathers had worked with my father for some years in the lab of a pulp mill in the Ottawa Valley. Although each of the men eventually went on to different jobs, the three families functioned thereafter like one large extended family. Any losses to this clan were felt by all of us who remained . . ."

PAT
(1915–2008)

He reaches the cottage after dark,
parks the car under birches
just beginning to leaf
and unlocks the building's door.
Seldom has he stood here alone.
Around him the main room is cluttered with
sixty years of family: a worn sleeping bag used as a quilt
tossed onto the daybed, a grandchild's toy locomotive
left on one of the dining table's benches,
paintings on the wall that show the cabin's dock
and White Duck Island a mile across the water
done long ago by a guest of one of the kids, shelves that hold novels
brought here by his wife, by visitors, and children's books
read to two generations. Dishes from the fall's last meal
stacked in the drying rack. Refrigerator unplugged,
well circuit breaker off. The large windows that face the lake
shuttered.

       Outside again, he
rummages under the deck
for a paddle and life jacket. He carries these
to the rocky shore
on a path between trees, then down
wooden stairs repaired and replaced
a dozen times. Above the storm line
he hauls from winter storage

his favourite of the two canoes: the oldest,
wooden ribbed and planked.

                    The water that buoys him,
that he cuts through, has low chop. He finds the remembered rhythm
infused in his arms and chest
and the craft gains speed
to a small regular slap of lake
against the prow. Few lights
are visible on distant headlands
this early in the season. No moon,
but a carelessly tossed, overarching myriad of
stars.

    In the steady pull
and lift forward of paddle,
body and mind disappear
with the muscles' shift, extension, release.
Night, canoe, who he was
merge into a moving vessel.

                  In the eastern lee
of the black-humped island, the water stills.
Stars fleck the surface
his paddle bends, resolves. The keel
he has become travels without thought
through liquid air. Above and around his passage,
his wake,
burn the universe's brilliant suns.

"A community, as well as a family, is diminished by a death. A community especially feels the absence of somebody who contributed a significant amount to ensure it functioned well . . ."

RICHARD MEISSENHEIMER
(1947–2006)

They lowered him into our valley earth
One August afternoon. After thirty-two years
Amid these streams, the rocky soil, the houses under the peaks,
His hands and wit

Will remain forever. A careful mechanic,
He knew how to assess fuel systems, when to coax
A reluctant alternator, when to hammer loose
A brake drum, when to rebuild, to weld,

To abandon. He never ceased to learn more
As the specs changed.
I wish I'd been a doctor,
He said. *Then I only would have to be familiar*

With two *models.*
He studied people closely as their cars,
A connoisseur of absurdities in either case
But never entirely dismissing hope

Concerning his neighbours. He sparked the unionization
Of a muffler shop where he worked in town
—Though they laid him off for the deed. He helped organize
Volunteer fire departments

Along the valley highway, served nine years as local chief
Then was pushed out by a district official
Who was a friend of neither justice nor safety.
The hands that kept us moving, the willingness to serve

That protected our homes, the droll words
That kept us laughing and focussed
Continue to float over his former acreage
By the river beach: the dawn mist that flows above the water

Late August to May
Transforming, as the day ages, into a cloud
That ascends the valley walls
To snag in the treetops
                    while below,

Vehicles he will never repair
Steer along the back road
Through all the seasons
He won't encounter now,

Like the faces unknown to him
Who will gather at potlucks
To dissect the latest area land use plan
And who assemble at the fire hall Tuesday nights

To run the pumper up and down our lanes
—His enduring presence a benediction
Hovering
In the valley air.

"Country or not, neighbours or not, peacetime or not, acquaintances and friends disappear as we age. Here are two poems about that . . ."

WHAT ABSENCE SAYS

—Raymond J. Smith (1930–2008)
and others

The chord dwindles to a single note
—a tone that remains drifting in air
like a puff of air, after silence

Such an extraction makes absence
corporeal
Along a mountain river
in February: smoky haze of
leafless cottonwoods
front a frieze of evergreens

White clouds streaming
swelling into a third of the sky

Ray's solemn, courteous drawl
Lynne's amused dubiousness: *Now, Tom,*
you don't really *mean*
Percy's lilting cadence

O fill that space
with hyacinth
lobelia, sunflower

Mount Cascade approached from the east
—its bulk striated with snow
in April: a rock so huge
its forested flanks become moss
halfway to the summit

and higher yet, lichen
then blank stone

—all I see
until the road turns

Each emptiness
reverberates under the bass of my days
while unheard treble sounds
shimmer like a stalk of
meadow fescue, stem of
aspen leaf

where the wind was

CONTROLLED FLIGHT INTO TERRAIN

For Gary Katz

How swiftly the wings ice:
wings the pallor of ice; the pilot's eyes
focussed ahead, or on instruments, maps, but the chill tumour

spreads suddenly across the wide structures
that buoy the vessel arrowing forward amid its engines'
steady sound, hiss of airframe parting freezing air

as a frost invisibly thickens: the drag of ice
first manifest in sluggish return from pitch
or yaw, but many things could cause this response. The silent unseen

insinuates itself onto flaps, rudders, each made heavier, slowed
molecule by molecule until the air
falters, cannot sustain lift, the wind of the vessel's passage

stills.
              He knew about moving air, breaths.
              When he edited a recorded interview for a program, he saved
              the sounds of the tiny intake of air

              that precedes each spoken sentence, then patched one set-aside
              noise before an excerpted statement to be used:
              the minuscule sibilance

              few are aware of, but without these breaths
              the abridged reply would ever so slightly jar in the ear.
              His skill at recasting speech, at crafting utterances, breaths

              that never were, matched his intense focus
              on talk: a painter who enumerates several colours
              in a green, the gourmet who isolates, tastes

cinnamon in a dish others only know as exquisite. "I don't
    want to
die," he said himself one afternoon in intensive care, but was
    reassured
he'd be home soon, the desired

words fading as in the tubes of an ancient radio, when my house
filled with the scent of silent peonies, nicotiana,
roses months away from the ice.

"Not only in a war zone do deaths on every side of us make us aware of our own mortality . . ."

FOR L.C.

Once they realized how quickly death is approaching
Some of my head hairs turned ashen-faced,
Others entirely white.

Like rats, hundreds of them
Have been abandoning the sinking ship
Of my body.

Now in rough weather
For the first time I feel death's cold hand
Pass atop my skull's skin.

"One school of thought sees all elegies as being, at some level, dirges for the author. There's no question that, for me, writing in response to the completion of the arc of someone else's life provides an opportunity to think hard about my own existence, with its mysteries and certainties . . ."

WASPS AND THE FIRES

I

The year brain and blood failed,
by early summer in our valley
small honeycombs of mud wasps
and the grey paper balloons of their kin
appeared in unusual numbers under eave soffits,
deck beams, and the limbs of the hazel trees
adjacent to the house. The yard swarmed
with dozens of the small yellow threats.

> One friend was newly ash
> when June's wet weather
> refused to show. Rivers
> withdrew into themselves
> exposing the stones and rocks of their course.
> Inside his skull, a fungus had previously thickened
> and spread
> into a huge callus, compressing
> lobe after lobe.

And the valley filled with smoke:
clusters of flame on the forested mountainside
north of Slocan—grey clouds from each flickering spot
merging into an immense plume. Another tattered grey mist
hazed a distant ridgetop
visible from my meadow by the lane.
Smell of smoke in the bedroom in the dark.

Taste of fire
always in my mouth. Wasps darting and hovering
through charred air

      into which another friend woke
      one hot morning
      discoloured by bruises:
      her blood laced with dribbles and clots
      of white. No corrosive poured into artery
      or ventricle
      could staunch what transformed her.

Death in the country is sudden:
a mound of feathers once a grouse
abruptly present amid the grass.
Tan blur of deer at the right front fender
as the road straightens from a curve,
then impact: a metallic crump.

II

All we speak, feel, accomplish:
stones piled by a hitchhiker
through long hours waiting on the shoulder of
a wooded downgrade. Structures of rock
balanced upon rock
lasting for months. The constructs
wiped away by the first snowplow.

      What existed before God
      decided to create the heavens and the waters?
      What prompted Him to suddenly
      devise a world?

Coastal, or inland
we live at the edge

of a swelling dark sea:
our days composed
of the intricate and noisy
pleasures and unpleasantnesses
of the port where we dwell
disputing and loving,
assembling the objects
that let us survive, and those by which
we define ourselves,
the sounds of our machines and music
crowding out
a relentless arrival of the waves.

The air here is salt, sharp amid the fierce gales'
stinging downpour
or in a gentler fall of water, or even below a clearing sky
in the afternoon: a blue soaring above
white peaks across the harbour.
Under that ocean
is black weather
devoid of every sense.

III

A shrill wail at these losses, this pain
—a sobbing from far within the earth
also grieving

Tears ascend through soil
toward light
As they flood forth

they blaze into flame
and are buoyed away by air
like particulates of ash

or insects

adrift
among these mountains

"I probably write too much about death. Yet one day I realized death isn't the only intense event regarding which I've written reams . . ."

DEATH AS A FAILED RELATIONSHIP

Death depicted as immanent
by the roadside, on the kitchen table
or under stars
and in thirty-seven elegies
that rail politely against
Dave, Shelley, parents
vanishing: fervent stacks of my words

that strike me now no different than
when a love I possess
is ended by someone else
and I brood over the syllables
of her name, the plan we had devised
to camp next summer from Rainy River
to the Gulf. I start to craft letters
to the withdrawn, hours of
details on why this abandonment
should not be happening, paragraph
after paragraph
of who did what after who said
they meant only
wouldn't it make more sense if
—seven or nine sheets
of single space
carefully folded and mailed
I could expect to hear back in only

Not a single cluster
of these words ever changed
a mind, restored or

brought relief,
let alone joy.

       Were they addressed
wrongly? Maybe death
is not responsible for this
agony, for my fear of
the abiding certainty
of a black void.
Perhaps the letters should have been sent
elsewhere: life,
who came on so sweetly,
is the one who chose
not to pursue its connection with
me, but instead
to return to its long-time marriage,
partnership with
What do I lack
as my letters beg to know
that a creepy, unsatisfying
—you said so yourself—
is preferable to *I know I have my*
faults, but

       Maybe despite
my many words, death is unaware
or at worst turns a blind eye
to the adulterous tease
it remains pledged to, couples with *I flinch*
whenever the phone How could life
I thought you told me initially be so
loving, warm *yet in the end*

"The dark of night, though, provides all too many hours for episodes of existential angst . . ."

MY GRAVES

Bed remade: sheets
pulled taut

while I curl toward
    a concrete enclosed platform

        waist high, crumbling pebbles and cement
        at one corner

        cracked open to reveal
        stacks inside of

        pastel coffins: cotton candy pink
        soft pale blue

        now water-stained, faded
        in blotches

My life reduced to
    the metal plate above on the concrete

        while in the dark box
        flesh, then bone

        frozen through the white months
        then thawed, heated

        repeatedly
Deathsick, gravesick

—pulled down into
     a black hole in a

space-time
  that not far from here

  will never have been

"In peace or war, one astonishing thing about dying is how completely we disappear as a personality, a being. The dead vanish, despite any of the pieties about how 'we will remember them,' or some once-important name becomes meaningless words on a public building. Even a memory we might have of the dead means nothing to them . . ."

THE QUESTION

Dense stand of aspen and pine,
trunk beyond trunk, some spruce,
lead up a hill without a name
Gaps between trees

form an untrodden passage, or nameless earth
is packed by hooves or clawed pads
among roots, old leaves, stones, with low grasses,
bearberry, juniper to either side

Into these openings
whatever *I* that I was named
become an exhalation of water droplets
will drift, dissipate: a mist

that failed to ask the right question
momentary amid the branches, the stir of air

CALLING THE SEASON HOME

"Poems, unquestionably, are for the living. Sometimes I see being alive as a bold adventure, as we squeak through our days avoiding—due to good luck or good decisions—threats that range from terminal disease to car crashes to, yes, bullets and bombs. Even parts of our bodies can be viewed as heroically staving off injury or worse . . ."

TONGUE

Daring inhabitant of a confined space
bounded by what can bruise, slice

or even kill the organ—a bilobate, blind, mouthless moray
lurking in a shark's maw, subsisting

on scraps gleaned from fangs
—darting between our incisors, canines, molars

with arrogant assurance. Or, because the tongue
is affixed to the floor of this slaughterhouse,

a blood-red sea anemone
without an oral fissure

waving among sharp rocks: a bifid flag of flesh
lurching and returning between white metal shards

mostly unscathed: snaps, whistles,
drone of the vibrating fabric

syllables of speech
and song

"The Afghan conflict is not the only aspect of our society that is mostly wrapped in silence. As I've elsewhere written, a taboo exists against an accurate depiction of daily employment, including how the hierarchical structure of most workplaces affects us both on and off the job.

"As one example of the taboo concerning work: in Ontario in 2007 the 401 freeway from Toronto eastward to CFB Trenton, where the bodies of Canadians killed in Afghanistan are brought back to this country, was renamed 'The Highway of Heroes' to honour the military dead conveyed to Toronto along that road. Yet more people were killed on the job in one year recently in just Alberta than Canadians were killed in all the years of Canada's participation in the Afghan civil war. Why are those who die as part of the forces of death and destruction automatically labelled heroes, while those who die to build their country are not?"

IF YOU'RE NOT FREE AT WORK, WHERE ARE YOU FREE?

Voices murmur concerning "a work/life balance"
or reverberate with conviction about
"our revered parliamentary heritage"
or intone why municipal tax subsidies are needed
to persuade someone to finance
a new mall. The words surge and drop and swell
like the fluctuating clamour of the drunken dinner parties
—symposiums—where the ebb and flow of wit
created the concept of democracy,
while around the guests
the lash, shackles, branding iron
ensured that grains and animals were raised
and brought to market, the meal was concocted
and served; locked windows and beatings
that resulted in broken limbs and teeth, permanent hearing loss
meant grapes were harvested, wine fermented,
bedchambers readied. Days, years of hopeless sweat,
the shattering of families

70

caused fresh flowers to be grown, cut,
arranged amid the company in vases
other slaves threw on wheels slick with wet mud
—flowers also placed
along the Senate's benches
in preparation for the next debate.

*"Not that human beings are ever satisfied with a subservient role, even
if they tolerate it for extended periods of time . . ."*

WHISTLE

Tunisia, Egypt, Canada

At the threshold of hearing:
a slight wheezy sound

almost inaudible when
   an entire shift, one hundred and twenty-five men and women
   —twelve of us with fifteen-year long-service pins
   and another thirty with ten-year certificates—
   are ordered to assemble in the lunchroom
   to be told by the human resources manager
   the company has taken away our jobs

A tiny background sibilance
   as somebody asks about the news report
   on the huge bonuses awarded the day before to the company's
     executives
   despite the fifth consecutive quarter of losses
   *If the corporation didn't offer this level of management
     remuneration,*
   we are informed, *it couldn't attract the best and brightest*

A faint tone
that from time to time seems drowned out by
official pronouncements of "labour peace" or
"truth and reconciliation," or by a local conglomerate's purchase of
a sports franchise, in support of which
you can yell, and spend your money on stadium tickets
or replicas of jerseys worn by those players receiving the largest salaries

Yet this muted whistling, always present,
can rise a few decibels

—as when no rice is available
or no water, or even when cutbacks to health services
necessitated by the need to finance an
international exposition, or overseas military excursion
mean the average wait in a bed placed in the jammed hospital
     corridors
before a patient can be moved to a ward
now stretches from four to six days
The low warbling becomes more shrill
     when a thousand men and women
     push into a hearing room to oppose
     the diversion of a river on behalf of a private contractor
     to generate power for a resort development

     The venture is approved
     regardless
and the noise splutters
almost to silence

But the steady thread of sound, commonly less than a whisper,
is a reassurance to many, an irritation to others,
a threat to a few

because there are also moments the whistle swells in volume
to a level people can't endure
     and run into the streets
     Some men and women clutch sticks
     with cardboard attached bearing words,
     and some carry sticks machined to
     clubs, or metal shafts fashioned into
     gun barrels

When the noise becomes entirely deafening
          certain men and women can't continue to stay any longer
          in palaces, or chambers of assembly
          This racket alters
          various domestic and community priorities

perhaps for a few days
or a decade

And if the tone subsides again
so wealthy individuals breathe relief
while the majority of us resume cursing the bus schedule
or the shift schedule
or the quality of the season's
new television offerings,
the whistle, though scarcely discernible,
perseveres:
the tinnitus of the world

"For much of my life, I made my living teaching in community and post-secondary educational institutions. In the latter, the classroom is frequently a site of conflict. After twelve years of compulsory *schooling, some students are in a feisty mood. And there is tension between the generations, between those with knowledge about certain matters and those who at least nominally seek to acquire it, and between those with a bit of power and those without . . ."*

STUDENTS FROM HELL

The ones who practise
aggressive comparison:
I'm getting As in all my other *classes*
or *Before I handed in my paper*
I read it to my friend in third year
and she *thought it was excellent*
or *Nobody taking different sections of this course*
has to do what you *require*

The student whose girlfriend
sitting beside him
receives better marks
So in class discussion he calls her ideas *stupid*

The blamer who tells you
your response to her work
is due to the inadequacies of a previous teacher
or because you dislike her
or her gender or style of dress

The victim who writes on your evaluation
This instructor lied
consistently all term, he may seem nice
but stabbed me in the back

And the sulkers
who pout in your office
while you try to show them your reasons
for their mark
who during class scrunch their faces in disgust
when you announce new reading or written assignments
who stage-whisper comments
and then sigh *Nothing* if you ask what they said
who look miserable
until they are back in the corridors with their friends again

"Instructors aren't shining angels either . . ."

TEACHERS FROM HELL

The professor who equates her pedagogical success
with her students' defeats: the more of them she fails
the more standards she has upheld

and hence the better teacher she is
The instructor who sets up office appointments
and then leaves notes to explain his absence

The one who assigns large amounts of reading
and just before the due date
announces this subject matter will not be part of the course

—thus penalizing only the conscientious
The teacher whose pedagogical goal is to be liked
The teacher whose pedagogical goal is to be hated

The instructor who is unprepared
and asks the class
What do you want to do today?

The professor who never gives As
because nobody is perfect

"Academics are easy to mock, especially those in universities. Graduate work—the apprenticeship process for academics—is affected by arcane procedures left over from the medieval origins of the institution. And fashionable academic beliefs, concepts that in some cases would result in forced hospitalization if uttered beyond the university's precincts, are regarded very seriously . . ."

HOW IT HAPPENED

They were friends in grad school:
nights arguing and agreeing about
discoveries of non-representational literary techniques.
Pretty soon, they had their own grad students
—not a lot, but over many years
these added up: every seven years
their incoming PhD students had
grad students, all articulate on why the writing
of their supervisor's supervisor, or
of their supervisor's friends, or of authors touched on
in their supervisor's thesis or their supervisor's friends' theses,
was worthy of a thesis
and of grants to support an account of how their words proved
the shortcomings of language, of material
literary production, of capitalism itself
according to critical theories whose thick prose
they had dog-paddled through in courses,
buoyed by the convictions of the instructor, and now
brought to their own classes in turn
as the essence of sophisticated, albeit hermetic,
analysis—which if untrue,
since nothing authored can be true,
was indispensable.

        Of course, only a handful of opportunities
to publish existed, since so many writers and editors
refused to abandon their dreary, outmoded

and politically reactionary compositional choices.
Yet a person could be assured of the hospitality of select journals
and book micropublishers, whose marginal status
represented further evidence of the oppositional quality
of the texts produced. And a person quickly became known,
especially with a recommendation. Although the same faces
constituted most of the audience at each public lecture or reading,
fresh boyfriends or girlfriends of crowd members
filled in a little, and a few of these newcomers even began
to show promise, applied to grad school,
crafted papers, organized conferences,
sat on panels, and defended, eventually,
their own thesis. In this manner
the world was saved.

"One positive aspect of universities is that they are that rare place in society where play with ideas is valued—regardless of the value of the ideas played with. For writers, such an activity can lead to puns. My previous book of poems High Speed Through Shoaling Water *had a poem in it called 'Teaching English' which played with the other meaning of that phrase. In that spirit, here's 'Writing Poetry' . . ."*

WRITING POETRY

I'm never sure what to say
even after an acquaintance of forty years.
Her letters to me are mostly down:
she's still not earning any money,
has been treated badly by this or that lover
—the affair launched with fresh excitement
but then he turns possessive, attempts to prevent her
seeing old pals, plus incidents of crazy jealousy occur
if she so much as mentions earlier boyfriends.
She appears attracted to control freaks,
though—as she'll acknowledge later—
they inevitably come on to her as the free spirits
she claims she prefers.
Besides anger management problems,
her partners frequently lose all interest in her
once the breakup happens.

She has issues with her family, too:
in and out of being the black sheep
among her siblings, a position she declares she prizes,
yet reading between the words
I'm conscious of how it hurts her.

                                            Long ago
I gave up offering advice
since I have my own relationship difficulties,
which in our correspondence

she never fails to inquire after
—one of the reasons
I've stayed in touch. Other friends of mine
shake their heads if I describe her latest disaster
or heartache. I'm often asked why I bother
keeping the connection.

                    Nice to hear
somebody's in more trouble than me,
I joke. In fact,
since the beginning I've believed a warm and generous soul
is confined in that hard-luck exterior.
And I do encounter people who tell me
she helped them at an intense moment
in their lives. Or maybe I continue to send her my news
and am pleased to scan hers
because I remember how gorgeous she was
when we first met. To envision her any other way
would be to admit my age, or how time,
while it deepens the love I have for her,
makes me more aware of her flaws
and their consequences, as well as more determined to be loyal
to that young heart
she spectacularly refuses to abandon.

"Lots of people I've known outside *the academy also love puns and other wordplay, especially when humour shakes up a listener's perceptions in aid of making a worthwhile point. One such person was Bruce 'Utah' Phillips, the Wobbly troubadour, who devoted much of his life to the struggle against oppression and war . . ."*

EXIT INTERVIEW: "UTAH" PHILLIPS

(1935–2008)—musician, organizer, traveller

Are you sorry to leave?

I feel I barely got started.

What do you consider your legacy?

Every act of kindness
and solidarity I did in the world.

Any regrets?

I'm sorry that people would rather listen to a song
than to sing themselves, let alone
make up their own tunes. I'm not talking here about adolescents,
who imagine they can use the music industry
to obtain glory and wealth. I mean how people used to sing together
as a family, and at parties, and at public meetings. In church
some still do, but we're mainly watchers now.
The union anthems, folk tunes, even pop songs
once were carried into the air on many voices
not just sung by one or, at most, a handful, while everybody else
listens, pays money to listen. Strict division of labour like this
was the *bosses'* idea, not ours: left to ourselves, we arrange a job
so those with the most skills show the way, while everybody else
joins in as best they know how.

But doesn't today's new media let people—

The rulers of this life are happy to have you shut yourself off
pushing at buttons on a computer keyboard
—thus giving the powers-that-be a free ride
in the real world. You can exchange virtual information by the hour
or hit "send" to add your name to another online petition
or denounce anything in your blog. That sound you faintly hear in the
    background
is the chortling of the ruling class: they've got you
exactly where they want you.

Wouldn't you agree, though, that—

Social change means face-to-face interactions with
your workmates, your neighbours, everybody who
shares the biosphere with you. With your head in a computer
you'll never figure out how you can put your values into effect
collectively with other live human beings
at your job site, or down the block, or in the union.

Would you say nostalgia played a part in your appeal?

I wish nostalgia entered into it. The boss still organizes the workplace
like it's *1805*, never mind 1905, or the twenty-first century.
He insists that the *money* the owners put into the enterprise
justifies his unelected right to tell you what to do all shift.
The boss might try to soften this arrangement by permitting
flextime, or by talking about starting a company daycare.
But when push comes to shove, it's you
who gets shoved. If the same rationale were applied
outside the office door or factory gate
only the rich would be allowed to vote. After all, they've invested their
    money
in this country or community, while you've only invested your
life. Everything I sang
and said was meant to celebrate each person who resists the idea

that, on the job or off, dollars trump decency, dollars
trump democracy. Would that the latter type of thinking
was so far in the past that at least a *few* people
could look back on it with nostalgia
—although the view of most of us would be: "Good riddance!"

How would you describe your contribution, then?

I carried it on: helped keep alive that age-old goal
to fashion a more human arrangement of society
than the present mess.
I saw revolutionary industrial unionism
as the best route to a world where we respect each other and
care for each other, including the homeless and other outcasts. After all,
it's through your and my daily *work*
that groceries are delivered to the stores,
kids are raised, roofs are shingled. The television and the newspapers
keep screeching at you *not* to pay attention to
how your employment keeps society functioning, and how your job
      affects
your life, and that of the people of your community, and the natural
      environment.
You're supposed to be concerned only about what happens to
a handful of celebrities, sports stars, politicians.
Yet it's our sweat and brainpower, not theirs,
that rebuilds the world each day.
The Wobblies—the Industrial Workers of the World—
knew back in 1905 that your life doesn't change for the better
because the team you root for wins, or because you buy something
you don't really need. Your life is improved
when your working day changes—when there's a real turnabout in
the power relations at your job, when there's a real change
in the impact the goods and services you create each shift have
on other people and on our planet.

How effective do you think you actually were?

I thought we'd be further along as a species by now.
Fred Thompson, a long-time IWW organizer, used to say
the working class always develops effective forms of resistance
about fifty to a hundred years behind the employing class.
I like to imagine we could be ahead of the curve for once.
In one way, we are: the IWW said in 1905 that world labour needs
a worldwide union. That was thinking "globalization"
long before the capitalists conceived of the term.
But the bosses are far in front of us when it comes to
putting the concept into practice. I don't doubt we'll get there
        eventually.
I just wish we weren't so damn slow.

Any parting advice?

If you can get out into the countryside
away from the smog and the noise and the money pollution,
you'll observe in the nighttime sky the three shining stars of the IWW:
Education, Organization, Emancipation.
Back in the city, if you look real hard on a clear day,
you can see those same three stars.

Where do you think you're going now?

I believe I will permanently achieve
what for so many years on tour
I demanded of my hosts who billeted me:
a bed
in a room
        with a door
                that closes.

"*Utah Phillips was perennially optimistic. But for me, much of the twenty-first century so far feels like a failure. I found it difficult to believe that after all the opposition to the Vietnam War forty years ago, US president George W. Bush could lead his country into another Asian military disaster—followed into the morass by his faithful lapdog, our own prime minister. The Iraqi War, like the Afghan War, was a frightening repetition of Vietnam-era government lying, waste of human lives and endeavour, and more evidence why imperialistic adventures hurt the people of the country undertaking them, as well as the invaded nation.*

"*Add in some consciousness of personal insufficiencies, perhaps an inevitable consequence of growing older, and I can find myself in a bleak mood . . .*"

SUSTENANCE

When I fail again

a huge cube of meat
fills my plate, a slab of steaming flesh

oozing red
that must be choked down, gobbets of fat

catching in my throat
until sucked clear at the last

instant, me gulping air
while the server

already proffers another chunk
balanced on a blade.

More, he demands, his tone
anticipating my acceptance.

So good.
Have more:

what you need.

"War brings not only death. Because some of the wounded don't die, we pay less attention to the suffering they endure on the road back to recovery, or to a much-altered or constrained existence. Like awareness of failure, dealing with pain is part of aging as well: convalescing from an operation, or experiencing one of those notorious back attacks . . ."

THE EVERLASTING ROOM

Red pain in a small room
That holds only me and pain.

Through a window
Green leaves spatter against green ground:

An image of some removed, pleasant place
Or hour. Within the room

Agony chooses what I do and
Can't: boss, captain,

Decrees the sole acceptable thought:
Priest, instructor.

Pain is an entire house
Compressed into a single room.

In this constriction, minutes are fractured,
Misshapen. Without possibility of measure

Music fails. Wine and carpentry
Never existed. Each memory torched,

Vaporized: a room of fear trembles
In the room of pain.

No wonder we forget the dead.
Dying in pain, they forget themselves,

Remember only pain's childhood,
Exams on pain, marriage

To pain: the body clamped to the anvil
Of pitiless time.

"All my life, I've never been sure if time is a friend or enemy. Time provides the space in which joy and accomplishment and beauty can appear and be savoured. Time also never stretches far enough to let me feel sated with the good things of life. Plus I know time includes evil, and time will destroy all I value—including me!

"When I first went to university, I never intended to be a poet. My goal was to be an astrophysicist. Second-year university math was my undoing: in those days, calculating the surface area of three-dimensional objects like a doughnut. I still retain a lay interest in cosmology, however, enjoying authors like Brian Greene, Steven Weinberg and Stephen Hawking. They observe that time appears to be the sole force in the universe that flows only one way. An equation—how we ultimately define nature—is, after all, about equivalences, and thus depicts a two-way *transformation.*

"Nobody seems to know why time alone is irreversible. All this thinking about time got me wondering what time would be like if it were more tangible. The next four poems wrestle with that notion . . ."

THE WOMAN WHO HEARD TIME

wouldn't specify the sound
she listened to. *Think tectonic plates,*
she said, *when they collide, there's subduction,*
right. One plate slides under the other?
The present, in a similar manner,
continually rides over the future.
Noise is vibration
and how could this moment not generate a tremor
as it pushes atop what was, until this second,
the next *moment. In string theory, too,*
the most elementary particles
are vibrating threads. That can't be silent.

Regardless of source, vibration
is motion in time. Thus time's clamour
is time hearing itself.

Time is the kitchen of the universe
and you bet there's a racket
where things are cooking. But the noise
can't be compared: not to a pulse
or faint tinnitus when the world is quiet.
What does a bell sound like
other than a bell?

THE MAN WHO COULD SEE TIME

The man who could see time
claimed it has a blue tinge
like a bruise, or meat beginning
to go bad.

       Its texture
that of a bale of straw
or a woven basket

except the intertwined stalks
fill all space—not drifting,
he said, but chockablock: the very stuff
of everything, although
permeable by each object,
including ourselves,
ordinarily perceived in three dimensions
despite existing also in the fourth.

String theory, he noted, posits
several other dimensions. He could not discern
those.

       He could see time
but he was looking for the soul.

THE WOMAN WHO TASTED TIME

announced: *Flakes of eggshell*
on your tongue, then coffee grounds.

Next: bits of cork
in a sip of wine.

Time's savour
is transitory

but always the not-yet
or after: scalding pepper in your mouth

as when you touch a lip
with fingers that prepared chilies,

then unripe quince, followed by
lemon rind.

THE MAN WHO COULD SMELL TIME

The man who could smell time
reported a scent resembling

licorice, or anise
and that the aroma was identical

regardless of the apparent motion
of the recipient of the olfactory impulse:

no change occurred in the odour's intensity or nose
when present transmuted to past

or future to now—
in other words, no Doppler shift.

This observation indicates,
the man insisted, time functions

neither as wave nor particle, but rather
as a constant, part of an equation

definitive of our universe:
relentlessly travelling

somewhere.

"New cosmological theories suggest time could eventually end, or that it is a human construct meant to explain changes in condition, rather than a force, dimension or other constituent part of the universe. For now, though, we are sure only that time moves in one direction: we can try to ameliorate the harm and destruction we as individuals—or our government—has caused in the world, but we cannot reverse such acts.

"Rural life, due to its closeness to a cyclical experience of time, appears to point to a different vision, of eternity continually revealed by the present."

NO END

October mist, and a black horse cantering
    along the fence line of a meadow
        under the mountains, prancing to a brief halt

where in the next field a small herd of other horses
    nibble grass, then the black horse spinning
        to gallop again along the foggy posts and barbed wire,

stretching neck and legs as though no end existed
    to this pasture by the river, so between one step and the next
        its hooves hammer down an earth road

formerly railway tracks, and thunder across rebuilt bridges
    onto long straightaways through a forest of fir, hemlock, cedar
        where saplings of cottonwood, aspen, pine

rise at the edges of the route that now curves
    past the sprawl of a farmstead—house, woodpile,
        maples and a spruce sheltering a pickup, tractor,

quad, and several chickens that have broken out of their pen
    —then fields once more, and woods, the black horse straining
        forward
            under low valley cloud, with the river

low and slow this season as the current skirts banks and islands
of leafless birches and cottonwood,
the dome of a willow that still flares yellow

and diminishes behind the horse that on the gravelled road
which, junction by siding by mainline, leads everywhere
I want to outrun time

"In the mountain valleys where I live, several eras collide. We can watch the latest news from Kandahar via satellite, but we heat our homes with wood. Party-line telephones were only replaced about a decade and a half ago. Few places in the area have cellphone reception. People's gardens—which of your veggies are having a particularly good year, and whether your fruit trees are affected by the epidemic of leaf miners—are a main topic of conversation between people. You'll hear far more talk about the berry crop and effective deer protection than about the officially approved subjects of corporatized sports, the latest TV shows declared significant and the misdeeds of the famous.

"Daily life in this region, more closely tied than an urban existence to weather and geography and to the plants and animals, seems more authentic than the life available to city dwellers. But despite the natural beauty on every hand, lives here have their own problems . . ."

THE CHILD WHO WENT INTO THE MOUNTAIN

In the drowsy evening light, two bears
shake the wooden posts and slabs
that protect the garden
just beyond the front porch of the mountain homestead. One bear
then the other
has reared awkwardly onto hind paws
and now shove their weight against the barrier,
rocking and tearing at it. Three more of their species
pace back and forth in the forest dusk
to the irregular thrum and creak of the bending uprights,
crack of a smashed plank.

                       Inside the palisade,
rows of corn stalks, leafy potato plants, and
lines of lettuce and onions await the moon.

                                 All that humans have built here
was carried up the switchbacked trail
from the valley town: load upon load,

year after year
strapped to packboards on the child and her parents
and secured to the donkey now anxiously circling in his pen
as the dark clouds of the bears
discover they have more leverage
if they rise to lean against the defences
in unison.

      Tonight the twelve-year-old is alone:
father employed in the next valley this season, mother
convalescing from back pain at a friend's in the village
closer to the local nursing station. The garden is winter food
this family needs no less than the bears
—much of it lately due to the child's toil
passing down the trail each morning to the valley road
where her bike is locked to a tree, until after school
she returns with groceries or
bags of fertilizer, or kerosene,
a set of drill bits. She hikes upward
carrying what she can, and guides the donkey
through the weather and the sunset
to the bottom again, to be loaded
and urged up the trail. Then tending her mother,
cooking on the propane burners
when the tank is not empty, otherwise the wood stove,
cleaning counters and floors, and on weekends
or a night without supplies to haul uphill,
hours of weeding.

      Outcry of rendered wood
as the shaking continues. The daughter
has loaded the rifle, her shoulder
remembering the pain of the weapon's kick
from when she fired it once before. The dark has thickened
but the swaying of the fence does not stop. She thinks
the boards of the gate are what are giving way,
points the rifle toward where she knows

the trail enters the compound.
In her mind she sees the face of the bear
most determined to break through: the face
of the lover, years later, who will injure her.

"Difficulties, hurts, losses and setbacks notwithstanding, we choose to make a life here . . ."

SMOKE

Accelerating past a snowbound fence
with dark lumps of cattle in the field beyond
munching hay strewn for them,
I flash by a plowed driveway, evergreen forest
behind the house, where from the chimney lifts
a plume of smoke

        as the candied scent
of burning stovewood fills the truck's cab
for a second or two

        like a pang of how much
I want to be four hours away,
opening the draft, scrunching paper and kindling
into the firebox, lighting the match

        so anyone
who drives down the back road will see
somebody in that place is at home.

"Although we appear to inhabit one of the most dysfunctional of centuries, where each day offers more revelations of misfeasance by corporate executives and government officials at every level, there is solace in being immersed in the round of the seasons. Fragile as these changes may be in the face of human destruction of the environment, while they occur they are a reassurance, even if each quarter of the year brings different challenges . . ."

THE TURN

In the shadows on the lawn
    below the clusters of mountain ash berries
        that—reddish-orange—now burden

the tree, in the moving spot of dark that paces
    chickadee and robin darting from birch leaves
        to maple, or the black speck

that hovers on the warm deck boards
    under the feathered spring of a hummingbird
        who releases his taut note beside the feeders,

the new season, piece by dim piece,
    accumulates chill air. Beneath tomato stems
        thickening through the hot afternoon, as under

the geraniums, the soil
    cools in the flakes of night. Shafts of darkness
        likewise lace the fir needles,

bank of cottonwood scrub. Squirrels
    frantically shake the hazel branches
        or streak across a fence rail

bearing in their mouths a green husk
    that hides a kernel of
        ice

to be hoarded below the new mulch of hazel leaves
    that have drifted against the lilac's trunk,
        that speckle the grass,

        that lodge among the marigold and gladiolus
    at the end of the irrigation sprinkler's cold spray
of summer

"The next poem describes an encounter with the annual arrival of the snow. I should mention that people who don't live in BC often confuse the Coast with the province, and will say things to me like, 'I bet you're glad to live where you don't have to shovel white stuff.' In fact, the inland mountain regions of BC are among the snowiest locations on the planet. The ski resort nearest my home is listed as one of the twenty snowiest ski hills on Earth.

"Yet even in this area, the first snowfall of the year is an occasion, as is the morning in September when one notices that the tops of the ridges across the valley have turned white overnight. At times, however, our choices or actions as well as nature's are involved in us reaching some moment of significant change . . ."

THE TOWN WHERE WINTER BEGINS

After the sawmill on the outskirts, steam ascending from
the drying sheds, I steer over a bridge and
onto streets where a wind riffles a blur of gilded leaves
downward across the pavement. In the shadows of houses,
lawns are tinctured with frost.
Many of the boulevard birch and maple
raise empty limbs to the afternoon.

I pause at a traffic signal
and see, in the next block, a dusting of snow
on roofs, sidewalks, a school parking lot.
Gearing up through the change of light,
I reach low white windrows left by the plow
along the shoulder. When the avenue starts to climb
to meet the tire dealership, recreation centre
and building supply that mark the town's farther edge,
a field shows an unbroken expanse of drifts.
Highway speed resumes up a grade,
and a passing lane starts that has not yet been cleared,
offering wheel paths only beside the sanded asphalt
that bears me up into the forest

where snow is matted and clotted on
spruce and fir limbs: tops bowed,
green branches outlined or bent by the clumps of white.
In a narrowing valley,
mountainsides on either hand
lift sharply through descending flakes
toward the overcast,
the desolate summit beyond.

"As the year ages into winter, we learn more about the landscape
that surrounds us: details and changes are revealed that the fecundity
on every hand has hidden from our sight. In the body politic, no less
than in our own lives, though, the passage of time is no guarantee of
increased knowledge, of wisdom. That's why it's good to have model
elders, who as they grow older continue to teach and inspire us . . ."

LEONARD COHEN DIDN'T GET ME LAID

Canada's Moaning Multi-Millionaire
Is back on tour at the age of eighty
Or eighty-seven—who can keep track?—
Monotoning on about how Annette, or was it Thalia,

Whose presence he once only wanted to worship,
Has been transformed into an agonizing memory.
Not a single lyric about
His business manager's efforts to assist him to attain

Detachment from earthly—and hence sensual—desire
By allegedly looting Mr. Rich Loser's bank account
While he was ensconced on his guru's LA mountaintop
Hoping to attain soul purification. Still, I must admit

The Perpetual Whiner represents an unexpected role model:
Women from several different decades at our bar table
All solemnly agreeing *He could do me anytime*
—With his advanced age apparently not a factor.

And me, being not quite so young myself as previously,
Probing *What's the appeal? The money*
He used to have? His songs about stay-up-all-hours suffering
Over some object of his attention? I don't understand it.

And the women, glancing at each other,
Smirk in a superior way and reply

Indeed. You could really learn *something*
From Leonard. And me insisting

I'm not opposed to acquiring
New information, even if I don't dye my hair
And never had plastic surgery. What, though,
Is that 'something'? Haughty laughter

And a few rolling eyes, as their conversation shifts to
How long ago they first heard about the concerts. The youngest,
Who looks about fifteen, though that can't be right
Since they check ID in this pub, starts an anecdote

About harassing her parents until her father
Ponied up the price of her admission.
Listen as I might, I glean no clue
From the women's continued gushes and sighs.

I stare into my beer and think
Another lonely night, with me growing poorer
—At these prices for drinks—and older
Without so much as a business manager.

"Despite the best efforts of politicians and corporate officials, we are drawn to the splendour of the authentic, the awe and wonder that—as the naturalist R.W. Sandford has noted—no television screen or other commercial artifice can truly provide. The brutality of war, and the odiousness of policies and products that isolate the individual from the commons and that put private profit above public good, cannot blunt our yearning for real connection with each other and with our astounding planet.

"The Chilean poet Pablo Neruda tells of how at the end of the Second World War, the first shop to open in devastated Warsaw was a bakery, and the second a flower store. Neruda's account echoes the title of the IWW union hymn in honour of a slogan from the 1912 Lawrence, Massachusetts, textile workers' strike: 'Bread and Roses.'

"Faced with the shambles those who rule us are making of the world, we look for what might heal us, restore our belief in a better future, provide the courage to continue to oppose until victory the destructive urge that is part of our species . . ."

CALLING THE SEASON HOME

I

Wisps of mist in the grey morning
stand upright on the river

while at the summit of a valley wall
larches scatter gold
across a green saddle

and a creek bed
along the foot of these peaks
waits for the snow
to cover freshly exposed boulders
and tree trunks stranded on gravel
Atop the stream's chill banks
cottonwood and birch limbs

are leafless
One alder, though
still radiates a fierce yellow cry
under slopes of balsam and pine
that rise toward cliffs
hundreds of metres above

II

A heart can absorb
entire October ranges like this
and not be ballasted down

Instead, even a spurt of dusty aspen leaves
lightens the organ

until it tugs free, lifts
over these canyons and forests

to ride the dark wind

like a raven
calling and calling
the season home

ACKNOWLEDGEMENTS

My thanks to the editors and staffs of the following journals and anthologies for their publication or acceptance for publication of poems (sometimes in earlier forms):

The Antigonish Review: Pat; Smoke; Students from Hell; The Summer Has Flared; Teachers from Hell; There Is No War, and You Would Not Have to Consider It If There Was; Whistle
Caliban Online: Sustenance
Canadian Literature: Adjustment
The Capilano Review: If You're Not Free at Work, Where Are You Free?; The Man Who Could See Time; The Woman Who Heard Time
CV2: Death as a Failed Relationship; Dirty Snow; The Grouse That Flew Underground; Tongue
Event: Highway 6, East of Slocan Lake, During the Afghan Campaign
Fiddlehead: Procession; The Town Where Winter Begins
5 AM: Air Support; How it Happened
Hubbub: Roses at the Grave of Summer; The Woman Who Tasted Time
The Iowa Review: What Absence Says
The Literary Review of Canada: Calling the Season Home; The Child Who Went into the Mountain; Writing Poetry
The New Quarterly: My Wounds
phati'tude: Interest